Contents / Index

Introduction

What could be nicer during the festive season than creating a feast for you and all your family and friends? In this book I have given you recipes for the traditional Turkey dinner including vegetarian alternatives and some more unusual festive fare ideas.

As you browse these pages, you will see I have included starter ideas, snacks for buffets, main courses, side dishes and not forgetting those important deserts! Oh, there's also chocolate and biscuit gift ideas.

All this should help you plan and deliver the perfect, stress free feast.

Have a fabulous time.

Paul x

Roast Turkey

If using a frozen turkey, always make sure it is thoroughly defrosted before cooking.

Take the turkey out of the fridge 1½ hours prior to cooking to allow it to reach ambient / room temperature. This prevents shock and assists cooking. Rub with butter and place in a roasting tin breast side down on a bed of onions, carrots, (neck & giblets if you have them) and celery. Put half a lemon inside the bird and season well.

For the last 30 minutes cooking turn breast side up.

Approx Cooking Times

As ovens vary, please ensure the bird is thoroughly cooked by testing the thickest part of the turkey with a skewer and check that the juices run clear. If they don't, return to the oven and cook for a further 15 minutes repeating this process until juices run clear. Always allow bird to rest for 35 to 55 minutes before carving. Cover the bird with tin foil and a couple of clean tea towels to keep it warm. As with any cooked food, ensure it is thoroughly cooked before eating. (Use cooking juices to make gravy page 6).

Cook first at 200°c or gas mark 6 for 25 minutes to seal then add the following time and temperature.

Cook whole bird at 180°c or gas mark 4.

4kg = 2hrs 30 mins	8kg = 3hrs 50mins
5kg = 2hrs 50 mins	9kg = 4hrs 10 mins
6kg = 3hrs 10 mins	10kg = 4hrs 30 mins
7kg = 3hrs 30mins	11kg = 4hrs 50 mins

All the following recipes state temperatures for a conventional oven, if you have a fan oven and it needs a lower temperature or less cooking time, please adjust accordingly as per manufactures instructions.

How Much Raw Meat to Buy

Whole Chicken and Turkey always allow 500g per person.
4kg Goose feeds 4 people
7kg Goose feeds 7 people
3kg Duck feeds 4 people
2kg Duck feeds 2 people
1 Quail feeds 2 people
1 Pheasant feeds 2 people
1 Pigeon feeds one person
Venison 180g lean meat per person
Leg of lamb (off the bone) 1.5kg feeds 4 people
Roast leg pork (off the bone) 225g per person
Roast beef (off the bone) 225g per person
Roast beef (on the bone) 375g per person
2kg fillet of beef feeds 8 people

Mushroom & Sherry Gravy

6 sliced Chestnut mushrooms
2 tbsp Sherry
300ml Chicken stock
1 tbsp Flour
½ tbsp Gravy browning
Residue meat juice from the turkey including neck and giblets if you have them (cooked around the turkey).
Pinch salt & pepper

1. Pour the turkey juices into a sauce pan or an oven dish that can go on the hob, including the cooked turkey neck and giblets, place over a medium heat so it starts bubbling add the mushrooms and cook for 5 minutes.
2. Sprinkle in the flour and mix well. Slowly add the stock (stirring all the time) then add the sherry, gravy browning and season.
3. Cook for five minutes, remove the giblets and turkey neck. Your gravy is ready to serve.

Yorkshire Puddings - serves 4-6

250 ml Milk
100ml Water
2 Eggs
175g Plain flour
Pinch salt
1 tbsp Vegetable oil or lard
½ Onion (peeled & finely chopped)
3 Rashers streaky bacon (optional)

1. Whisk the milk, water, eggs, salt, flour to a smooth batter.
2. Chop the bacon and add to the batter with the onion. Stir with a spoon.
3. Pour the oil into 5 muffin moulds and heat in a preheated oven at 230°c for 5 minutes. (You can use smaller moulds to make more Yorkshires if desired).
4. Once heated, remove from the oven and pour the batter mix evenly into each mould.
5. Place back into the oven at 230°c for 25 - 35 minutes until cooked. Be very careful when adding the batter to the hot oil, as it spits.

Vegetable Bake - serves 4

1 Courgette (sliced)
1 Onion (sliced)
2 Carrots (peeled & sliced)
¼ Swede (peeled & sliced)
¼ Butternut squash (sliced)
1 Medium potato (peeled & sliced)
1 Sweet potato sliced (peeled & sliced)
3 Cloves garlic (finely chopped)
150ml Double cream
Chicken or vegetable stock cube mixed with 100ml boiling water
1 tsp Mixed herbs
Salt & pepper
100g Cheese (grated)

1. Layer all the vegetables into an oven proof dish placing the garlic and season between the layers.
2. Mix together the cream, herbs, stock, and pour over the vegetables.
3. Sprinkle over ½ the cheese, cover in foil and bake in the oven 1½ hours at 160°c.
4. Remove the tin foil, add the rest of the cheese and bake for a further 30 minutes, and serve.

Pigs In Blankets - serves 4

8 Chipolatas
8 Slices streaky bacon
4 Dates (stoned & halved)
4 Dried apricots (stoned & halved)
3 Sage leaves (cut into 3 strips)

1. Place a chipolata on a slice of streaky bacon. Then put a date and apricot either side with a sage sliver on top. Roll up to make the pig in blanket. Repeat this process to use all the ingredients.
2. Cook in an oven proof dish in the oven at 250°c for 12 minutes, turning after 6 minutes. or cook in the Halogen oven on the low rack as per recipe.

Roasted Vegetables **- serves 4**

1 Medium potato (peeled)
¼ tbsp Oil
1 tbsp Mayonnaise (full fat)
Pinch salt & Pepper
2 sprigs Rosemary (picked)
1 clove Garlic (chopped)
¼ medium Swede (peeled)
1 small Parsnip (peeled)
1 medium Beetroot (peeled)
1 Carrot (peeled)
½ Onion (peeled)

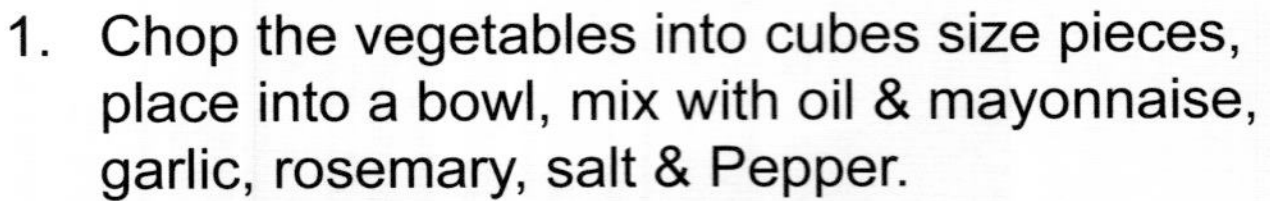

1. Chop the vegetables into cubes size pieces, place into a bowl, mix with oil & mayonnaise, garlic, rosemary, salt & Pepper.
2. Place on a oven proof dish into a pre-heated oven or Hot Air Fryer and cook for 20-30 minutes at 170°c, stirring occasionally if needed.

Carrots

You can boil the carrots in boiling water, but add a cupful of orange juice, a tbsp of sugar and the zest of an orange to give them an extra sweet flavour. Drain and serve.

Brussel Sprouts

Boil them in the usual way. Fry off some chopped streaky bacon and some ready cooked chestnuts, mix in the cooked Brussel sprouts and serve.

Red Cabbage **- serves 4**

½ Red cabbage (finely sliced)
1 Apple (cored, peeled & chopped)
1 Cinnamon stick
1 tbsp Marmalade
1 tbsp Cranberry sauce
2 tbsp Sultanas
1 tbsp Vinegar
6 tbsp Water

1. Mix all the ingredients together and place in a pan on a medium heat. Bring to the boil, then cook on a low heat for 25 minutes until thoroughly cooked. Or place in a hot air fryer for 25 minutes adding a little extra water during cooking if required.

Brandy Sauce - serves 4

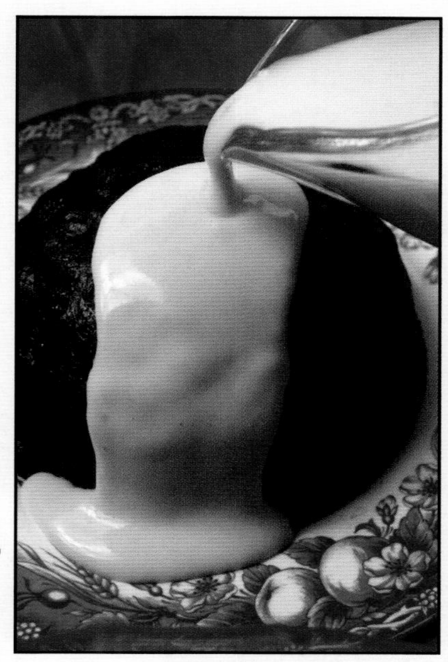

500ml Warm Milk
200ml Double cream
2 tbsp Brown sugar
50g Butter
2 tbsp Brandy
1 tbsp Golden syrup
1 tsp Vanilla essence
2 tbsp Plain flour
½ tbsp Marmalade

1. Melt the butter in a pan, then add the flour and cook out for 2 minutes stirring continuously.
2. Gradually add the warm milk on a medium heat stirring continuously.
3. Add the cream, golden syrup, marmalade, vanilla, brandy and brown sugar.
4. Bring to the boil, simmer for 5 minutes and serve.

Cranberry sauce - serves 4

300g Cranberries (fresh or frozen)
100g Light brown castor sugar
½ Lemon juice
13g Butter
1 tbsp Port (optional)
1 Orange (zest & juice)
2 tbsp Water
25g Sultanas (optional)

Mix the water, lemon juice, orange juice & orange zest and sugar in a pan. Bring to the boil. Add the port, sultanas, butter and the cranberries. Simmer for 6 minutes. Cool and place in the refrigerator. Serve chilled.

Roast Potatoes - serves 4

5 baking potatoes (peeled and cut into large chunks)
2 tbsp vegetable oil
2 tbsp duck or goose fat
2 tsp yeast extract
2 sprigs rosemary
Salt & pepper

1. Boil the potatoes for 10 minutes, drain and shake in the pan.
2. Mix the yeast extract with the duck or goose fat with the vegetable oil and 1 tbsp boiling water.
3. Place the potatoes in a roasting dish coat in the oil mixture and place in a preheated oven 220°c for 45 minutes turning after 20 minutes. Add the rosemary sprigs to the pan for the last 10 minutes of cooking.

This can be cooked in the Hot Air Fryer but pre boiling method 1. is not necessary.

Top Tip!... If prefer, you can use parsley instead of coriander.

Carrot & Coriander Soup

Ingredients **Serves 4 - 6**

4 Carrots (peeled & sliced)
1 Potato (peeled & cubed)
1 Onion (peeled & sliced)
50g Butter
2 tbsp Coriander (roughly chopped)
1 litre Whole milk
1 Vegetable stock cube mixed with 500ml boiling water
Pinch salt & pepper

Method

1. Put the butter, onions, salt and pepper in a large pan, medium heat and cook without colouring for 5 minutes.
2. Add the carrots, and potatoes, continue to cook for a further 5 minutes.
3. Add the stock and boil for 15 minutes. Add the milk, simmer for 5 minutes.
4. Add the chopped coriander.
5. Blend and serve.

This can be made in a Multi-Cooker

Top Tip!... You can also use savoury cooked minced beef / lamb or sweet mince as an alternative filling.

Feta & Dill Parcels

Ingredients **Makes 10**

270g Filo pastry
200g Feta cheese (crumbled)
½ Red onion (finely chopped)
2 tbsp Dill (chopped)
Pinch salt & pepper
50g Butter
13g Melted butter for brushing

Method

1. Mix together the onion, Feta, dill, salt and pepper in a bowl.
2. Lay the pastry out and cut into squares. Take one of the squares and place another on top at a 45 degree angle.
3. Repeat once more. (See pic).
4. Place a spoonful of the Feta mix in the centre, moisten the edge with a little water and pull up the corners to make a parcel. Repeat this process 9 times.
5. Brush parcels with melted butter.
6. Pre-heat the oven and oven tray to 250c and place the parcels onto the tray. Turn oven down to 170°c. Cook for 10 minutes until golden brown.

These can be made on the low rack of a Halogen Oven.

Top Tip!... This is great served with cheese and cold meats.

Jewelled Beetroot

Ingredients **Serves 12**

12 Cubes Blackcurrant jelly (1x125g pack)
4 Cooked medium beetroots (diced)
3 tbsp Malt vinegar
2 Pickled onions (chopped)
250ml Water
Pinch salt & pepper

Method

1. Dissolve the jelly in 100ml of boiling water for 1 minute. (Either in the microwave or in a pan on a medium heat).
2. Add the remaining cold water along with vinegar, beetroot, onions and seasoning, stir well.
3. Allow to cool, place in the fridge to set.
4. Once set, mix before serving.

You can use a Multi-Cooker to make this instead.

Top Tip!... As an alternative, you can serve this as a mushroom and cheese risotto.

Mushroom Risotto Balls

Ingredients

Makes 24

250g Arborio rice
1 large Onion (chopped)
2 Cloves garlic (finely chopped)
1 tsp Mixed dried herbs
1 tbsp Olive oil
25g Butter
250g Chestnut mushrooms (cleaned & sliced)
50g Parmesan cheese
1.2 litres Chicken stock
125ml White wine
125g Mozzarella (chopped)
Pinch pepper
Vegetable oil
6 slices White bread
400g Flour
5 Eggs

Method

1. Put the onions and olive oil in a pan and fry for 10 minutes.
2. Add mushrooms, garlic and herbs and fry for a further 5 minutes.
3. Add the Arborio rice and combine.
4. Slowly, add the stock and wine. Continue cooking until it is absorbed and the rice is cooked, stirring all the time.
5. Stir in the Mozzarella, Parmesan and butter.
6. Season and remove from the heat transfer to a bowl. Once cooled place in fridge to chill for 2 hours, until the risotto is firm.
7. Put the bread in a food processor to make breadcrumbs and place in a bowl.
8. Beat the eggs together in another bowl.
9. Take the chilled risotto and roll into 5cm balls then roll in the flour then the egg and finally the breadcrumbs. Repeat with all the balls. Heat the vegetable oil in a large pan and shallow fry until golden brown.

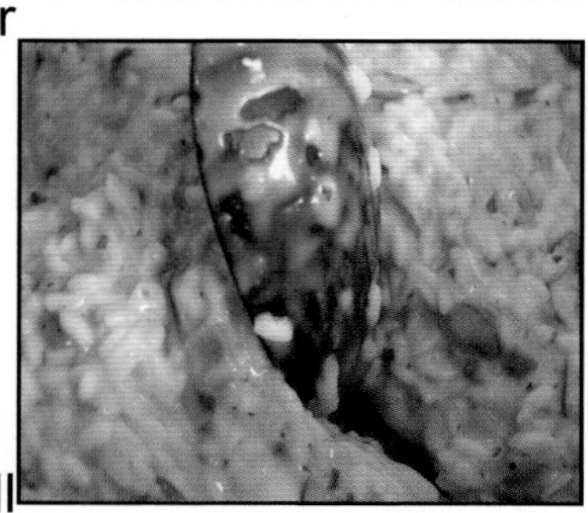

You can use a Multi-Cooker to make this instead.

Top Tip!... Wonderful served with cold meats
or cheese at a buffet.

Pineapple Chutney

Ingredients **Serves 6**

425g Tinned pineapple or fresh
(drained & chopped, keeping the juice)
2 tbsp Sweet chilli sauce
4 tbsp Caster sugar
2 tbsp Malt vinegar
1 Small onion (finely chopped)
1 Clove garlic (finely chopped)
Pinch salt & pepper
¼ Vegetable stock cube mixed
with 1 tbsp boiling water.

Method

1. Place the sugar in a non stick pan over a medium heat. Cook until it starts to go a golden colour, then carefully add the onion and turn the heat up to high.
2. Add the garlic, keep stirring and cook for a further 1 minute.
3. Add the chopped pineapple and cook for another 2 minutes.
4. Add the stock, malt vinegar, sweet chilli sauce, salt & pepper and cook for 6 more minutes adding some of the pineapple juice as necessary to form a thick syrup consistency.

You can use a Multi-Cooker to make this instead.

Top Tips!... For a vegetarian option, leave out the ham. Can be made in a Halogen Oven on low rack as per recipe, or deep fried in oil.

Prosciutto Ham, Mozzarella & Sundried Tomato Bread Balls

Ingredients **Makes 12-14**

275g Strong flour “00” Grade
½ tsp Salt
1 tsp Caster sugar
12g Butter (melted)
150ml Warm milk
13g Fresh yeast or 7g dried
4 Slices prosciutto ham (chopped)
120g Sundried tomatoes in oil (60g net weight)
20 mozzarella mini balls (halved)
1 tbsp milk to glaze

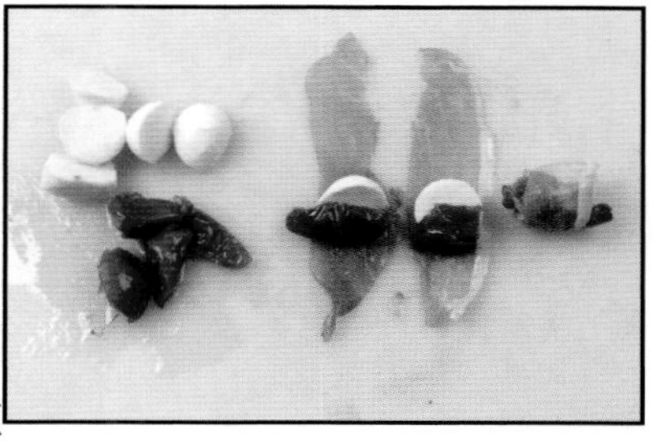

Method

1. Mix in a bowl the yeast with milk and sugar, leave for six minutes.
2. Place flour and salt into a bowl and stir in melted butter. Add yeast mixture. Mix to a soft dough.
3. Knead dough for ten minutes until it becomes firm and elasticised (stretchy). This can be done in a food mixer with a dough hook.
4. Put dough into a bowl and cover with a clean damp cloth. Leave in a warm place for ten minutes, until the dough has risen.
5. While this is rising, wrap the sun dried tomato with half a mozzarella ball in a piece of ham.
6. Knead the dough again for two minutes to reduce it to the original size. Roll into balls and make a hole inside them. Place your wrapped ham, sundried tomato and mozzarella in the hole. Fold the dough back over the hole to encapsulate the filling.
7. Allow to rest in a warm place for 10 minutes, glaze with milk and bake in the oven at 220°C for 15 to 25 minutes or until thoroughly cooked.

Top Tip!... **These can be made all year round; lovely at picnics . You can also make in a Halogen Oven on low rack with extender ring as per recipe.**

Pork & Cranberry Sausage Rolls

Ingredients **Makes 36-38**

425g Puff pastry
2 Small onion (finely chopped)
450g Pork sausage meat
2 tbsp Cranberry sauce
½ tsp Mixed herbs
Pinch salt & pepper
1 tbsp Sesame seeds
1 Egg to glaze

Method

1. Mix together sausage meat, herbs, onion, cranberry, salt and pepper in a bowl.
2. Roll out puff pastry to 3mm thickness and cut into 4 long strips. Approx 12cm x 30cm.
3. Place a pastry strip on a greased baking tray, then roll some sausage meat mixture and place on the strip. Glaze edge and fold pastry over the top.
4. Score the top and cut into sausage rolls.
5. Glaze the top with egg and sprinkle with sesame seeds.
6. Bake in a pre-heated oven at 200°c for 12 minutes or until golden brown and thoroughly cooked.

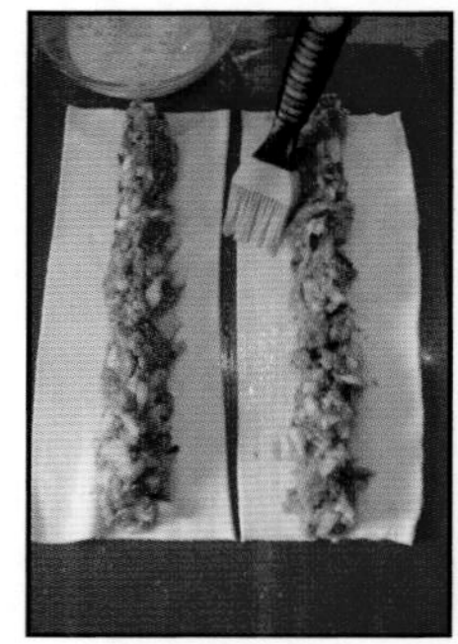

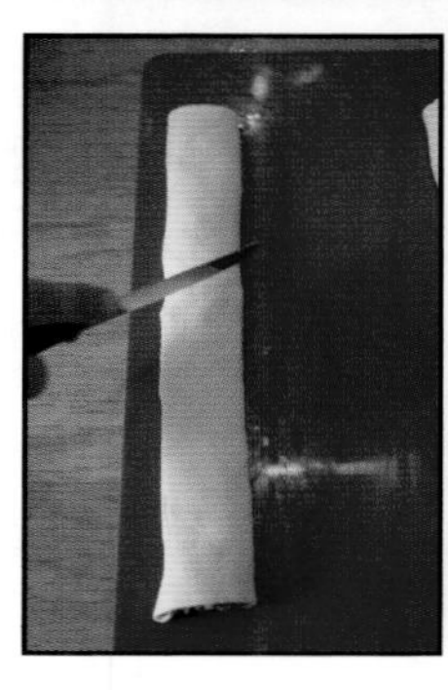
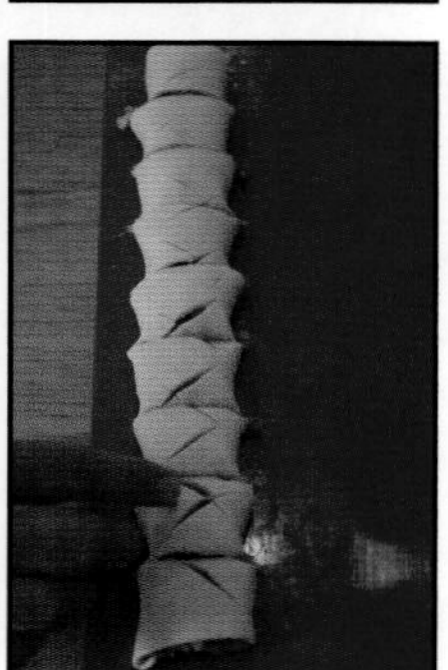

Variations
1. Instead of the cranberry, add 1 Apple peeled and finely chopped and one tablespoon of sweet pickle.
2. Add 5 chopped medium mushrooms to the sausage meat.
3. Use stuffing mix mixed with grated cheese and grated carrot instead of sausage meat.

Top Tip!... This can also be served with traditional MaryRose or thousand island sauce instead.

Salmon & Crab Tower

Ingredients **Serves 4-6**

125g Smoked salmon (chopped) (can use trimmings)
170g White crab meat (tinned or fresh)
4 Fish sticks (diced)
Pinch salt & pepper
8 Tiger prawns
1 Lemon
1 tbsp Chopped parsley
1 Ripe avocado (peeled & diced)
1 tbsp Mayonnaise

Sauce

½ tsp Cumin
1 tsp Vinegar
1 tbsp honey
Squeeze lemon juice

Method

1. In a bowl mix together mayonnaise, fish sticks, white crab meat, smoked salmon, avocado, parsley, salt, pepper and a squeeze of lemon.
2. In a separate bowl, mix together the cumin, vinegar, honey and lemon juice to make the sauce.
3. Place a spoonful of salmon mixture on the centre of a starter plate (or in a mould); place two prawns on top.
4. Serve with a spoonful of the sauce around the edge of the plate.

Top Tip!... Try using cooked broccoli instead of watercress; just add the broccoli when you add the stock.

Stilton & Watercress Soup

Ingredients

Serves 6

75g Stilton cheese
90g Watercress
1 Potato (peeled & diced)
1 Apple (peeled & diced)
1 Onion (peeled & diced)
300ml Chicken or vegetable stock
400ml Whole milk
50ml Double cream
Pinch salt & pepper
25g Butter

Method

1. Fry the onion in a pan with the butter, apple and potato, for 5 minutes without colouring.
2. Add the stock and bring to the boil. Simmer for 10 minutes with the lid on.
3. Add the watercress and season.
4. Add the milk and cream, bring to the boil; reducing the heat and crumble in the Stilton.
5. Remove from the heat, blend and serve.

You can use a blender or stick blender for this recipe.

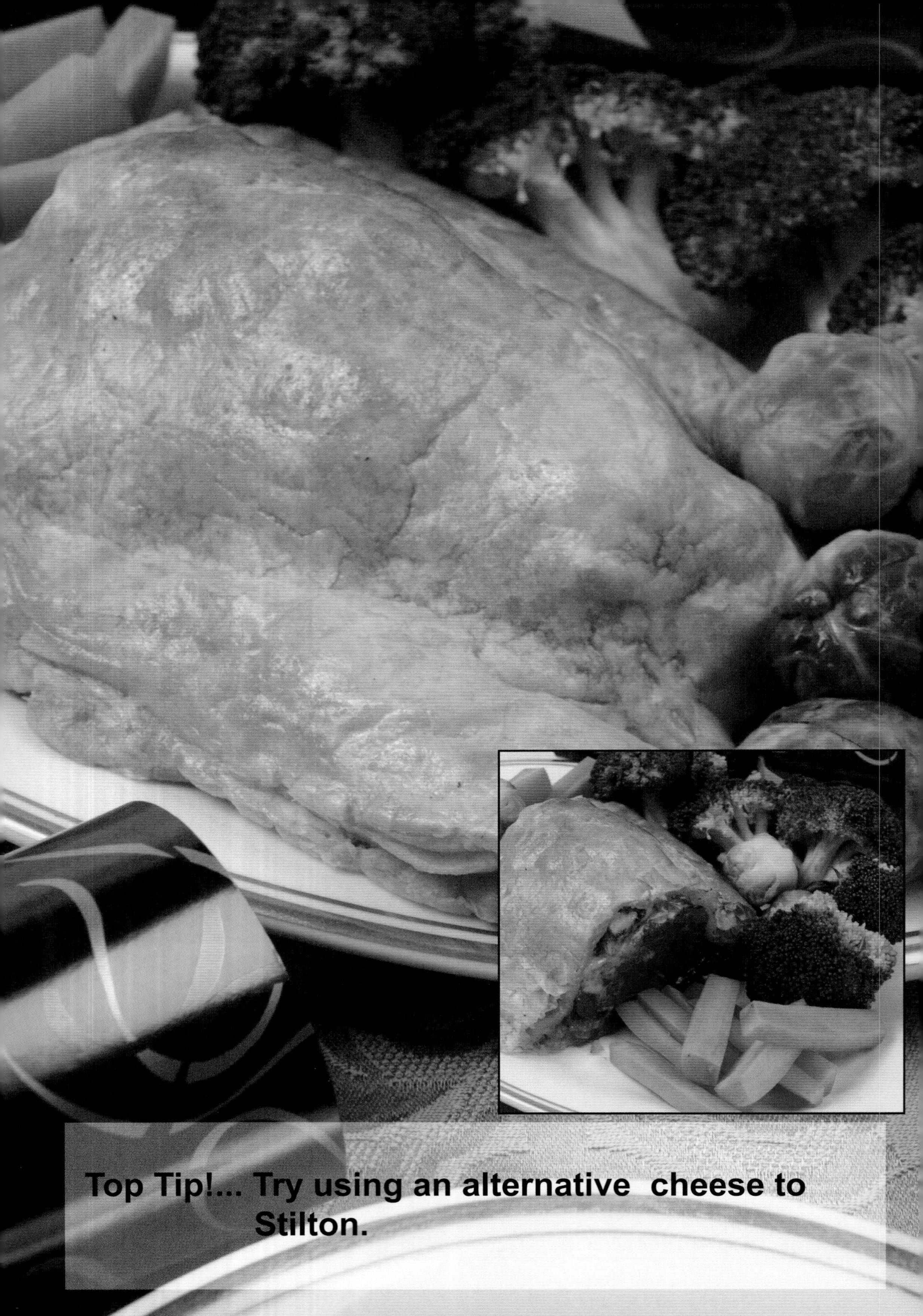

Top Tip!... Try using an alternative cheese to Stilton.

Beef Wellington with Stilton & Walnut

Ingredients **Serves 2**

112g Puff pastry
75g Stilton or blue cheese
300g Fillet beef
1 Red onion (sliced)
1 Egg
6 Walnuts
15g Butter
Pinch salt & pepper

Method

1. Roll out the pastry to a 20x24cm rectangle and cut into 2 equal parts 20x12cm.
2. Place one piece of the pastry onto a baking tray and cook in a pre-heated oven at 250°c or gas mark 9 for 5 minutes.
3. Place the onions and beef onto the pastry and cook at 200°c: rare 2 minutes, medium 5 minutes and well-done 7 minutes.
4. Add the Stilton, walnuts and the last layer of pastry. Glaze with the egg and cook for a further 15 minutes.

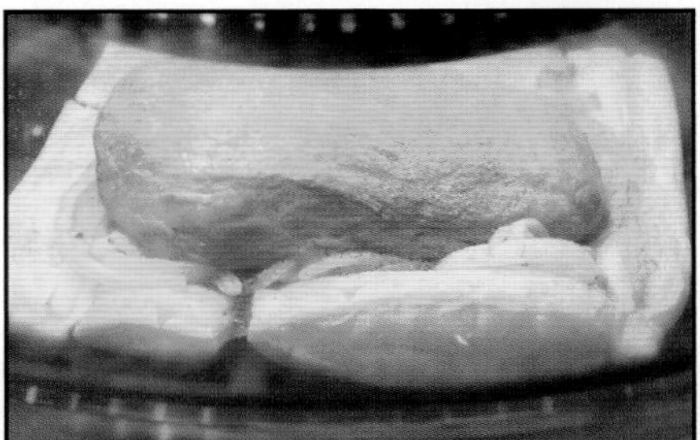

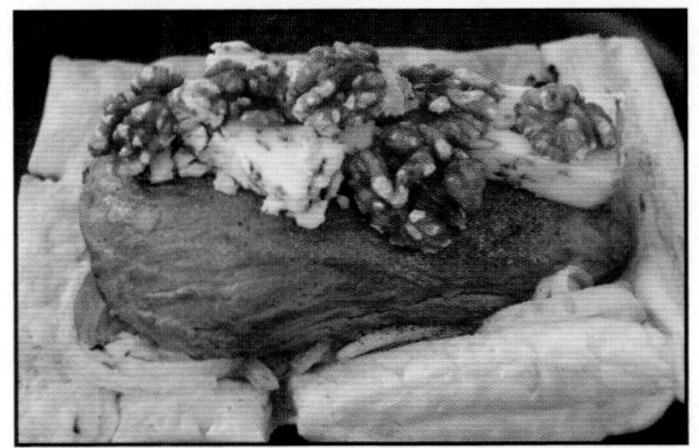

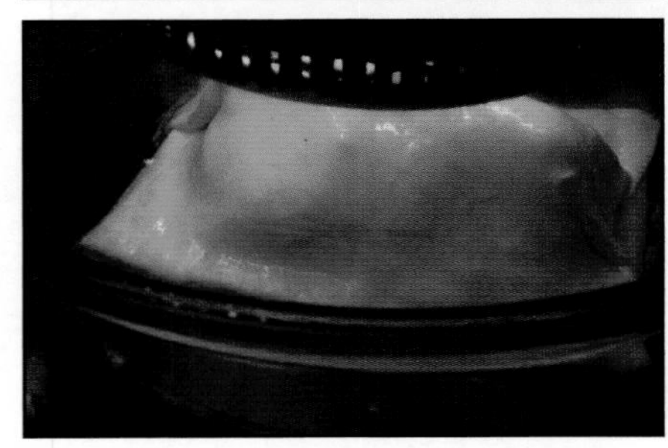

You can use a Halogen Oven, cook on the round tray on the low rack, as per recipe.

Top Tip!.. If you like your stuffing sweeter, try
adding 1 tbsp cranberry sauce to
the mix.

Chicken & Duck with Cherry Stuffing

Ingredients **Serves 3-4**

6 Fresh cherries
1 Pork sausage (skinned)
65g Sage & onion stuffing mix
13g Butter
Pinch salt & pepper
6 Slices streaky bacon
2 Chicken breasts
1 Duck breast
Cooks string
Kitchen foil

Method

1. Put the sage and onion stuffing mix in a bowl with 100ml of boiling water and mix. Add the sausage meat and combine with the stuffing.
2. De-stone the cherries and cut into quarters and mix with the stuffing.
3. On a large sheet of foil lay the streaky bacon out next to each other (see pic). Cut the butter into pieces and put over the top.
4. Place the duck breast and two chicken breasts on top of the bacon then fill with the stuffing and season. Roll up, tie with the string then wrap with the foil.
5. Bake in the oven 200°c for 1 hour 25 minutes. Allow to rest for 20 minutes (in the foil) and serve.

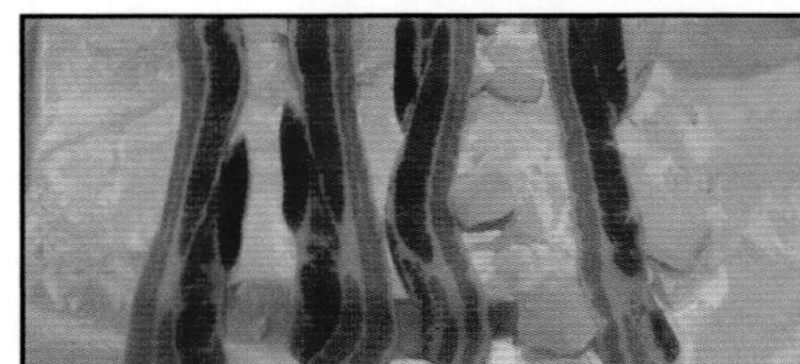

You can use a Halogen Oven on the low rack, as per recipe.

Top Tips!...This is so juicy and can be cooked any time of the year. You can also cook in a Halogen Oven on low rack as per recipe.

Chicken & Lamb with Honey and Mustard

Ingredients

Serves 3-4

2 Chicken breasts
240g Lamb neck fillet
1 Pork sausage (skinned)
4 Slices Prosciutto ham
2 tbsp Sage & onion stuffing mix
13g Butter
2 Cloves garlic (chopped)
2 tbsp Honey
1 tsp Mustard
1 tbsp Chopped fresh parsley
Pinch salt & pepper
Kitchen string
Kitchen foil

Method

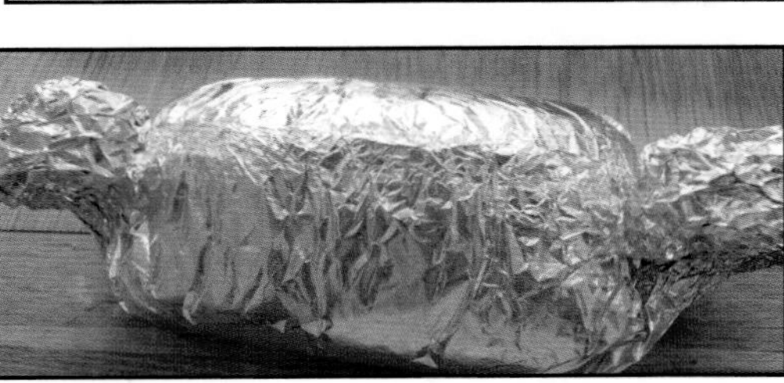

1. Mix together butter, garlic, parsley, honey and mustard in a bowl.
2. In a separate bowl put the sage and onion stuffing mix with 100ml of boiling water and mix. Add the sausage meat and combine together.
3. On a large sheet of foil pour the honey and garlic mixture in the centre. Lay the Prosciutto ham out in lines over the top (see pic).
4. Place the lamb and two chicken breasts in a line then fill with the stuffing/sausage mix.
5. Roll up, tie with the string then wrap with the foil.
6. Bake in the oven at 200°c for 1 hour 20 minutes. Allow to rest for 20 minutes (in the foil) and serve.

Top Tip!... Serve with the
onion bread sauce (See page 41).

Cola Gammon

Ingredients **Serves 4-6**

1.2 kg Gammon
(soak gammon in fresh water over-night in the refridgerator if you want to remove more of the salt content before cooking)
1 Orange in segments
1 Onion studded with 6 cloves
6 Cardamom pods
3 Cloves garlic
2 Litres of cola

Method

1. Place all ingredients into a slow cooker for 8 hours (or 45 minutes in a pressure cooker; on full pressure). If using a pan, bring to the boil then simmer with lid on for 3½ hours. (Do not allow to boil dry; top up with more water if necessary).
2. Drain and serve. You can also allow to cool. Refrigerate and serve cold.

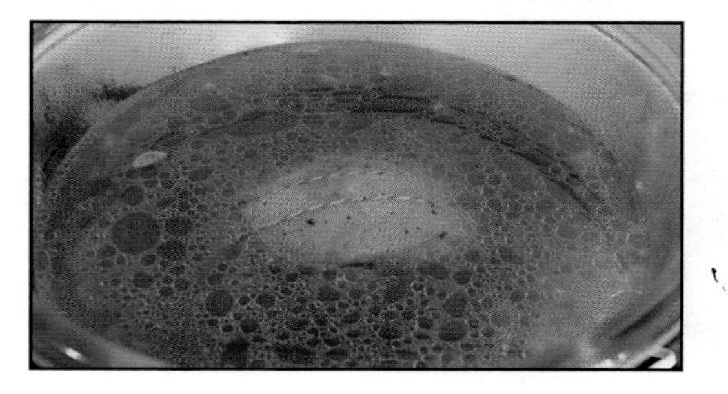

If you want to make it a glazed gammon, once cooked, cover in honey and place on the low rack in the Halogen oven at 250°c. for 10 minutes.

Top Tip!...Use 200g sliced fillet steak to create a
delicious Beef Stroganoff.

Mushroom Stroganoff

Ingredients

Serves 4

250g Chestnut mushrooms (quartered)
1 Yellow pepper (De-seeded & sliced)
1 Garlic clove (peeled & crushed)
75ml Double cream
½ Medium onion (sliced)
1 tbsp Olive oil
1 tsp Dijon mustard
1 tsp Cornflour mixed with 25ml water
2 tbsp Sherry (sweet or dry)
1 Chicken stock cube mixed with100ml boiling water
1 tsp Dark soy sauce
15g Butter
Pinch salt & pepper

Method

1. Put the mushrooms, onion, peppers, garlic, olive oil, salt & pepper in a bowl and mix thoroughly.
2. Pour into a hot pan and fry for 10 minutes.
3. Add the butter and cook for a further 5 minutes.
4. Put the mustard, cream, soy sauce, sherry, cornflour and stock in a bowl and mix. Add to the other ingredients and stir. Bring to the boil and simmer for a further 10 minutes, or until thoroughly cooked.

You can use a Multi-Cooker or Hot Air Fryer to make this instead, as per recipe.

Top Tip!... Try making a nut Wellington by following Beef wellington recipe on Page 29 and substituting beef with Nut Roast.

Nut Loaf

Ingredients **Serves 4**

125g Mushrooms (sliced)
50g Cashew nuts (chopped)
100g Mixed nuts (chopped)
75g Quinoa
90g Dried bulgur wheat
1 Vegetable stock cube mixed with 500ml boiling water
2 Slices whole meal bread (chopped into bread crumbs)
100g Plain flour
2 Small onion (finely chopped)
1 Sweet potato (peeled & finely diced)
50g Butter or oil
4 Cloves garlic (finely chopped)
1 tsp Mixed herbs
2 tbsp Cranberry sauce
Pinch salt & pepper

Method

1. Fry the onion with 40g butter in a pan for 2 minutes on a medium heat.
2. Add the mushrooms and cook for 2 minutes.
3. Add the garlic, quinoa, bulgur wheat and cook for 2 minutes.
4. Add the stock and cranberry. Season and stir, bring to the boil and simmer with the lid on for 10 minutes.
5. Add the sweet potato and cook for 5 minutes.
6. In a separate bowl, mix together the flour, nuts and breadcrumbs. Add this to the other ingredients and stir together.
7. Pour into a greased loaf tin, put 10g butter and 2 tbsp water on top. Bake in a pre-heated oven at 180°c for 15 minutes.

Top Tip!...Delicious with gammon or sausages.

Onion Bread Sauce

Ingredients **Serves 6 - 8**

1 Large onion (finely chopped)
3 Slices white bread
150ml Double cream
600ml Whole milk
1 Chicken stock cube mixed with 100ml boiling water
2 tbsp Sage & onion stuffing mix
¼ tbsp Thyme
25g Butter
Tiny pinch ground cinnamon (optional)
Pinch salt & pepper

Method

1. In a food processor, blend the bread to a fine breadcrumb.
2. In a pan, sweat the onions with the butter for 5 minutes.
3. Add the breadcrumbs, cream, milk, stock, stuffing mix, thyme, cinnamon, salt and pepper.
4. Stir and bring to the boil. Simmer for 5 minutes.
5. Blend with a stick blender and serve.

You can use a Multi-Cooker to make this instead.

Top Tip!... Replace the pineapple with chopped peaches.

Pork Stuffed with Gammon

Ingredients

Serves 4

1.2kg Pork joint
330g Gammon steak (cut in two)
200g Tinned pineapple pieces in juice
85g Sage and onion stuffing mix
Pinch salt & pepper
Fresh parsley

Method

1. Add 100mls of boiling water to stuffing mix and stir. Add the pineapple and mix.
2. Cut open the pork joint so that it is almost into two pieces; but still held together by the fat.
3. Place the gammon pieces in this gap (each side) and fill with the stuffing. (See pic).
4. Roll up and tie with butcher's string. Rub skin with salt.
5. Place in a hot oven at 250°c for 30 minutes then turn down to 200°c for 1hr 30 minutes or until thoroughly cooked.

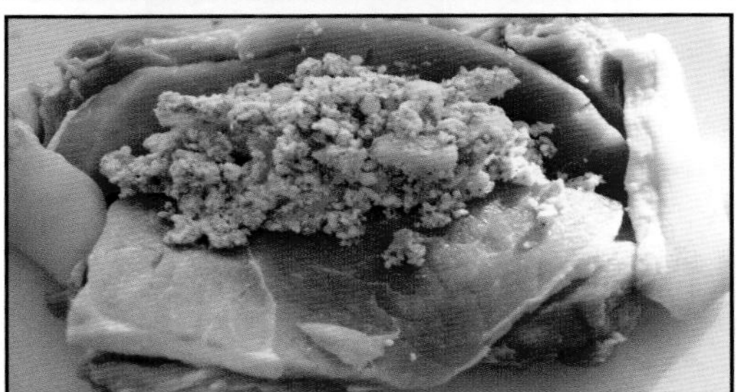

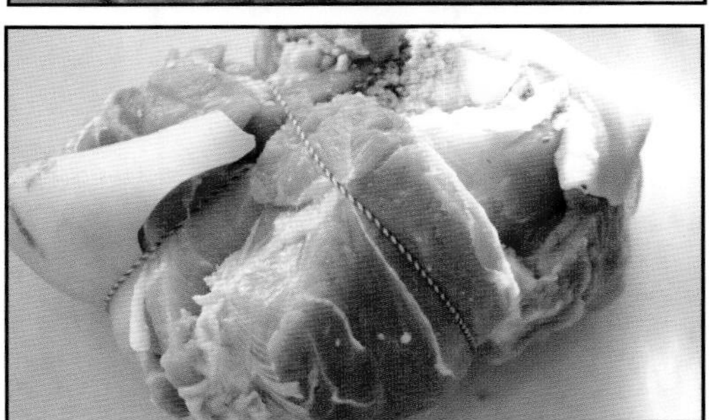

Can be cooked in a Halogen oven on the low rack with the extender ring, as per instructions, turning over the joint every 30 minutes.

Top Tip!...You can make this a vegetarian curry by replacing the turkey with different vegetables.

Turkey Curry

Ingredients

Serves 4

400g Cooked turkey (chopped)

Curry sauce

1 Onion (finely chopped)
1½ tbsp Vegetable oil
1 Clove garlic (crushed)
1 Cooking apple (peeled, cored and chopped)
1 Chicken stock cube mixed with 600ml boiling water
50g Dates (stoned & chopped)
25g Curry powder
1 tbsp Plain flour
25g Butter
1 tbsp Mango chutney
½ tsp Soy sauce
50g Dried apricots (chopped)
1 tsp Sweet chilli sauce
4 tbsp Double cream
Pinch salt & pepper

Method

1. Fry onion and curry powder in butter and oil for 4 minutes on a medium heat.
2. Add apple and cook for a further 5 minutes.
3. Add garlic, salt, pepper and fry for a further 2 minutes.
4. Stir in flour.
5. Slowly add chicken stock whilst stirring and bring to the boil.
6. Continue to stir as you add the mango chutney, soy sauce, sweet chilli sauce, dates and apricots.
7. Add the leftover turkey and cream, bring to the boil.
8. Turn down, cover and simmer for 35 minutes.

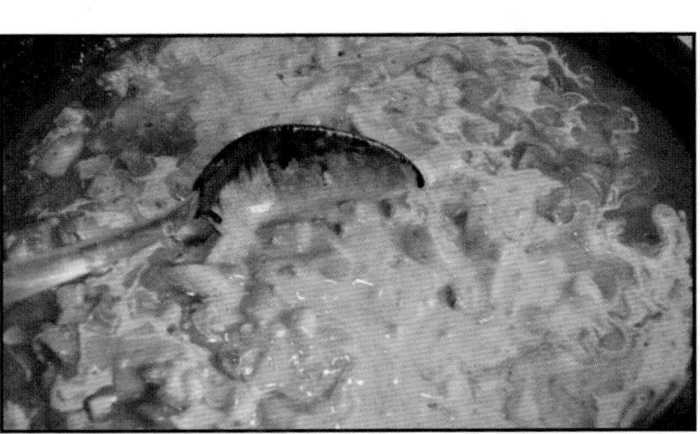

This can be cooked in a Multi-Cooker or Hot Air Fryer.

Top Tip!... You can use cooked chicken instead of turkey.

Turkey Pasta

Ingredients **Serves 4**

215g Cooked turkey (chopped)
1 Onion (chopped)
1 tbsp Olive oil
2 tbsp Cranberry sauce
2 tbsp Mayonnaise
300g Penne pasta
Pinch salt & pepper
Fresh parsley (chopped)

Method

1. Cook the penne pasta, drain and cool in cold water.
2. In a pan fry off the onion with the oil (medium heat) for 3-4 minutes. Allow to cool.
3. Thoroughly drain the pasta and mix together with the onions, turkey, cranberry sauce, mayonnaise, parsley, salt and pepper.

You can use a Multi-Cooker or Hot Air Fryer to fry the onions.

Top Tip!... You can use readymade short crust
pastry to save time.

All Butter Mince Pies

Ingredients **Makes 12**

Short crust pastry
400g Plain flour
200g Cold butter (cut into cubes)
A little cold water
2 tbsp caster sugar
Pinch salt

Filling
150g Sultanas
150g Raisins
150g Mixed dried fruit
75g Glace cherries (halved)
2 tbsp Cherry brandy
2 tbsp Port
50g Brown sugar
25g butter
25g mixed peel

Method

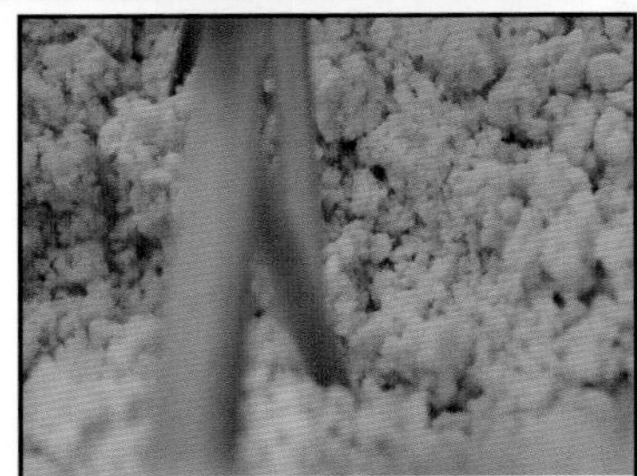

1. For short crust pastry, put flour, butter, sugar and salt into a food processor. Blitz until it looks like fine breadcrumbs. Then add cold water, a little at a time until a dough is formed. (This will leave the sides of the mixing bowl clean).
2. Allow dough to rest (wrapping in cling film for 30 minutes).

3. In a pan put the sultanas, raisins, mixed fruit, glace cherries, cherry brandy, port, brown sugar, butter and mixed peel over a medium heat and cook for 7 minutes.
4. Roll out the pastry and use to make tart bases. Place a spoonful of filling in each and then place a lattice on top.

5. Bake in a pre-heated oven at 175°c for 15-20 minutes.

You can make the filling in a Multi-Cooker or Hot Air Fryer. These are great re-heated in a Halogen Oven.

Top Tip!... You can use fresh berries instead of frozen.

Berry & Port Terrine

Ingredients

Serves 6

24 cubes Blackcurrant jelly
(2x135g pack) or sugar free jelly
450g Fresh or frozen berries
3 tbsp Port
1 tbsp Caster sugar or sweetener
400ml Water
40g Fresh redcurrants
Fresh mint

Method

1. Dissolve the jelly in 150mls of boiling water in a microwave for 2 minutes.
2. Add the sugar and port to the melted jelly and stir.
3. Using a loaf mould, place the frozen berries inside and pour over the jelly mix.
4. Transfer to the freezer for 15 minutes.
5. Transfer to the refrigerator to continue to set.
6. Decorate with redcurrants and fresh mint.

Delicious served with the ice cream bombe page 63.

Chocolate & Cherry Log

Ingredients

Serves 6

Chocolate Log
4 Eggs
100g Self-raising flour
100g Caster sugar
3 tbsp Cocoa powder
10g butter for greasing

Filling
410g Cherry pie filling
3 tbsp Cherry brandy (optional)
50g milk Chocolate (grated)

Frosting
3 tbsp Gravy browning
300g Butter (room temp)
100g Cocoa drinking chocolate
300g Icing sugar

Decoration
50g Walnuts & redcurrants

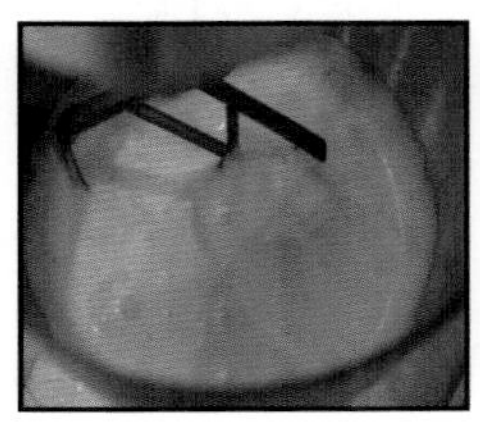

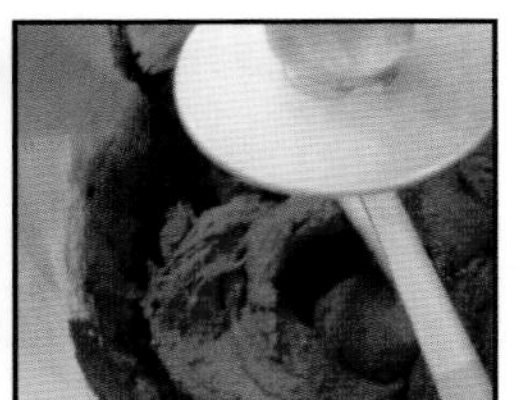

Method

1. Line a baking sheet with greaseproof paper and grease with butter.
2. Pre-heat oven to 180c (fan oven), 200c (regular) or gas mark 6.
3. With an electric whisk, mix the sugar and egg for 7 minutes until light, fluffy and pale.
4. Mix together the flour and cocoa and sieve over the egg mixture slowly folding in with a metal spoon.
5. Pour this on to the prepared baking sheet and place on the middle rack of the oven for 10 minutes.
6. To make the frosting, mix together the icing sugar, butter, gravy browning and cocoa in a bowl, whisk until light and fluffy.
7. Once the sponge is cooked, remove from the oven, place a piece of buttered grease proof paper on top and roll up. Allow to cool.
8. Mix the cherry pie filling with the cherry brandy and grated chocolate.
9. Once the sponge is cool, unroll, remove greaseproof paper and spread the cherry pie filling mix over the top. Roll once again then cover the sponge with the frosting and decorate.

Take the hard work out of the preparation with a food mixer.

Top Tip!... You can add 100g mixed unsalted nuts to the cake mixture.

Christmas Cake

Ingredients

Serves 12

800g Mixed fruit
60g Glace cherries
4 tbsp Dark rum
2 tbsp Cherry brandy
250g Plain flour
1 tsp Mixed spice
250g Butter
250g Dark brown sugar
25g Almond (ground)
5 Eggs
2 tsp Gravy browning
Zest of 1 orange
50g Mixed peel
1 pack Ready to roll marzipan
1 pack Ready to roll fondant icing
2 tbsp Apricot jam

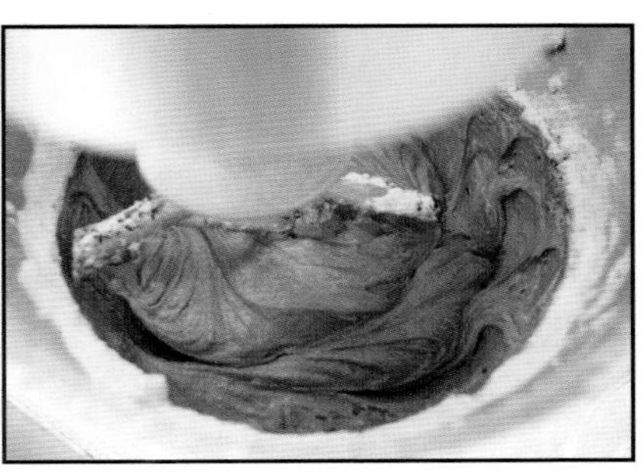

Method

1. Put the mixed fruit in a bowl and pour over the cherry brandy and rum. Cover and set aside. (This can be prepared the night before).
2. Line a 20cm round or 18cm square cake tin.
3. Pre-heat the oven to 150°c (fan), 160°c (regular) or gas mark 2½.
4. In a mixer, cream the butter and sugar until light, pale and fluffy.
5. Beat the eggs in a separate bowl and very slowly add to the creamed butter and sugar whilst mixing.
6. Add the flour, ground almonds, mixed spice, gravy browning and slowly fold into the mixture.
7. Add the mixed fruit, glace cherries, mixed peel and orange zest.
8. Spoon the mixture into the pre prepared baking tin and bake for 3 hours.
9. Test to see if the cake is fully cooked by popping a knife in the middle of the cake. If it comes out clean, the cake is ready. If not, give it a further 30 minutes of cooking.
10. Store in a cool place wrapped in grease proof paper in a sealed container. (you can feed the cake with alcohol)
11. When you are ready for your cake cover in apricot jam, marzipan and icing.

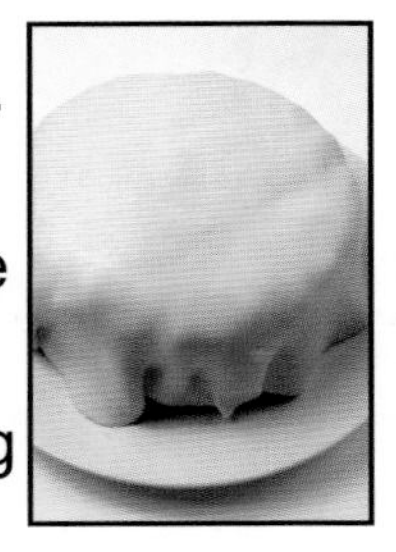

No Added sugar Christmas Cake

Ingredients

Serves 12

1kg Mixed fruit
75g Almond (ground)
50g Pecan nuts (chopped)
125ml Apple juice
125ml Pineapple juice
250ml Vegetable oil
300g Wholemeal self-raising flour
2 tsp Mixed spice
1 Fresh apple (grated)
1 Carrot (peeled & grated)
2 Medium bananas (sliced)
2 tbsp Unsweetened or low sugar marmalade
1 tsp Vanilla essence
4 Eggs
1 Lemon (rind & juice)
¼ Cup brandy

Decoration

Dates ,dried apricot, hazelnuts, cashew nuts, unsweetend marmalade

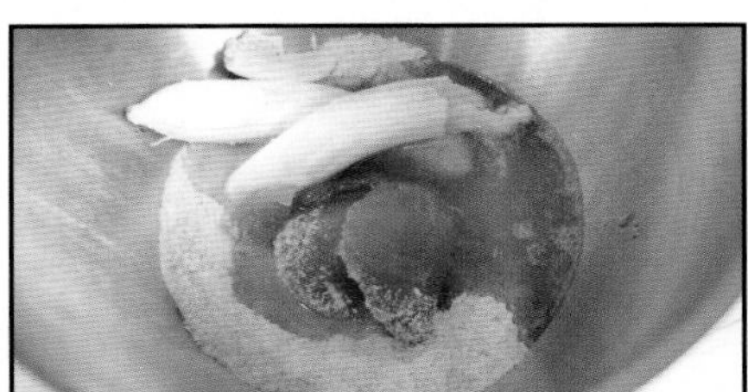

Method

1. Soak the mixed fruit, lemon peel, vanilla, and brandy with the pineapple and apple juice for 2 hours.
2. In a food mixer, mix the flour, oil, banana, marmalade, apple and carrot.
3. Slowly add the eggs, and then slowly add the fruit.
4. Pour into a lined 20cm cake tin.
5. Bake in oven for 3 hours at 150°c (fan), 160°c (regular) or gas mark 2½.
6. Once cooked, remove from the tin and cool. Decorate with dates, apricots, unsweetened marmalade and nuts.

Please note: there is a high natural sugar content in this cake.

Top Tip!... Serve with brandy sauce. (See recipe on page 9).

Christmas Pudding

Ingredients **Serves 6**

1 Eating apple
(peeled, cored & grated)
100g Raisins
175g Luxury mixed fruit
75g Dark candied cherries
75ml Brandy/cherry brandy or rum
(I use half cherry brandy, half rum)
1 Carrot (peeled & grated)
Juice and zest of 1 orange
2 Eggs
62g Suet (vegetable or beef)
1½ tbsp Black treacle or gravy browning.
100g dark Muscovado sugar
75g Fresh breadcrumbs
¼ tsp Nutmeg
¼ tsp Mixed spice
1oz Pecan nuts (optional)
1oz ground almonds (optional)
10g butter for greasing

Method

1. In a bowl put the apple, raisins, mixed fruit, candied cherries, brandy/rum, carrot, juice/zest of orange, eggs, suet, treacle, sugar, breadcrumbs, nutmeg, mixed spice, pecans, ground almonds and mix together.
2. Put the mixed ingredients in a greased 2 pint pudding basin.
3. Cover with a circle of grease proof paper then tin foil (if boiling).
4. Place in a saucepan 3/4 submerged in boiling water with the lid on and cook for 5 hours. Top up with water as necessary. Alternatively, cook for 6-8 minutes in microwave using cling film instead of foil.
5. Allow to cool, in a cool dry place to keep the pudding ready for the big day.

You can add more brandy if required by putting a tablespoon of brandy or rum under the grease proof paper allowing it to soak in slowly, (amount depends on your taste).

Top Tip!... Great idea
as a gift.

Coconut & Jam Cookies

Ingredients **Makes 25**

250g Butter
150g Light brown sugar
1 Egg (yolk & white separated)
½ tsp Mixed spice
175g Flour
175g Ground almonds
Zest of 1 lemon
3 tbsp Raspberry jam
10 tbsp Desiccated coconut

Method

1. In a bowl mix the butter, brown sugar, lemon zest together. Add the egg yolk. Slowly add the flour, ground almonds and mixed spice to make a dough.
2. In a separte bowl lightly beat up the egg white and put on a plate.
3. On another plate put the coconut.
4. Roll the dough into small balls.
5. Roll dough balls in the egg white and then roll in the coconut.
6. Place the balls in a greased jam tart tin.
7. Make an imprint in the middle of each ball with your thumb or the end of a wooden spoon and fill with jam.
8. Bake at 200°c for 12-15 minutes.

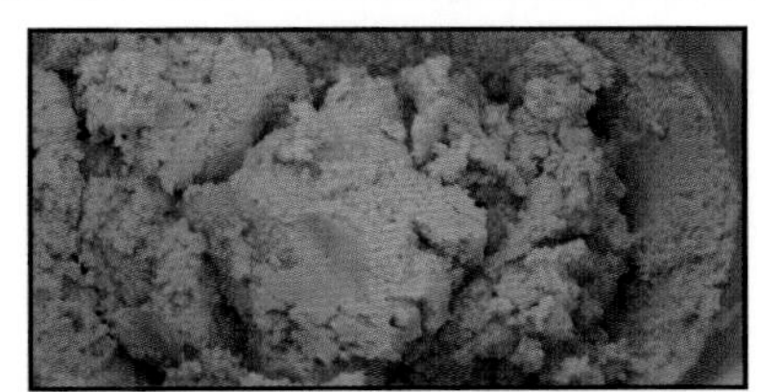

Take the hard work out of the preparation with a food mixer.

Ice Cream Bombe

Ingredients

Serves 6

2 tbsp Rum
1¼ litres Double cream
125g Mixed dried fruit
50g Dried cranberries
2 tsp Custard powder mixed with a little cold water
125g Caster sugar

Decoration

Walnuts
Redcurrants

Method

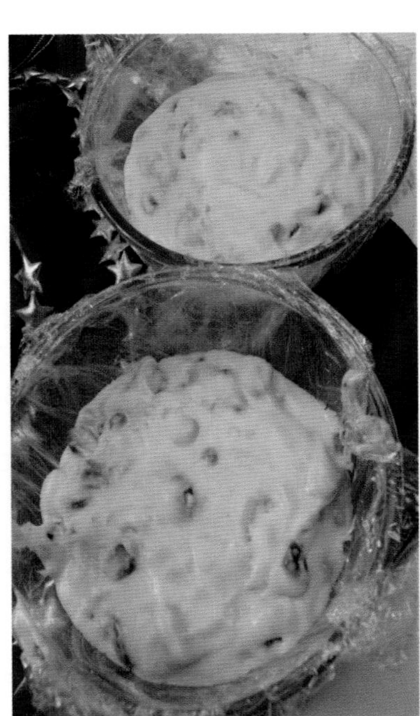

1. Put the rum, double cream, mixed fruit, cranberries and caster sugar in a pan. Bring it to the boil and simmer for 5 minutes.
2. Mix the custard powder with a little water, add to the cream mixture, bring to the boil whilst stirring and cool.
3. Grease two 750ml pudding basins and line with cling film. Pour equal amounts into each, leave till cool. Place into the freezer for at least 24 hours.
4. When you are ready to serve, remove the ice cream from the basins, push together to make a ball and serve with walnuts and redcurrants.

You can use a Multi-Cooker to make this instead.

Top Tip!...Fun to make all year round. Try using desiccated coconut on the outside instead of cocoa.

Wheat Biscuit Truffles

Ingredients **Makes 18-20**

4 Breakfast wheat biscuits
4 tbsp Chocolate nut spread
150g Sweetened condensed milk
4 tbsp Rum or whole milk
2 tbsp Cocoa
75g Crushed hazel nuts

Method

1. Crush the wheat biscuits into a bowl, then add the condensed milk, rum and combine. Add the chocolate nut spread, mix together, cover and let stand for 2 hours in the refridgerator.
2. Roll into small balls, roll balls in the crushed nuts and in the cocoa powder. Place in the freezer for 10 minutes.
3. Place in the refrigerator until you are ready to serve.

Mulled Wine

1 bottle Red wine
1 Orange (sliced)
1 Lemon (sliced)
200g Dark brown sugar
1 Apple (halved studded with 5 cloves)
1 Cinnamon stick
1 cm square fresh ginger (peeled)
Optional – 2 tbsp
Cherry brandy, orange liquor or sloe gin
Place all ingredients in a pan and simmer for 20 minutes. Do not boil, as the alcohol will evaporate. Can be made few days in advance and stored in the refrigerator. Reheat prior to serving in a pan or a slow cooker.

Books Available In Our Range

If you have any questions regarding the recipes in this book, please feel free to visit my website:

www.paulbrodel.co.uk

or email us at: **cook@paulbrodel.co.uk**